SCHOOL ACCOMMODATIONS

SCHOOL ACCOMMODATIONS

*A Parent's Guide to
the 504, the IEP
and to
Every Child's Legal Right
to a
Free and Appropriate
Public Education
in the
Least Restrictive Environment*

Mari Hoashi Franklin
Attorney at Law

School Accommodations:
A Parent's Guide to the 504, the IEP, and to Every Child's Legal Right to a Free and Appropriate Public Education in the Least Restrictive Environment.

Copyright © 2018 by Mari Hoashi Franklin. All Rights Reserved.

All rights reserved. No part of this book may be reproduced in any form or by any electronic or mechanical means including information storage and retrieval systems, without permission in writing from the author. The only exception is by a reviewer, who may quote short excerpts in a review.

Mari Hoashi Franklin
Visit my website at www.MariFranklinLaw.com

Printed in the United States of America

First Printing: October 2018
Mari Franklin, Attorney at Law

ISBN-13:9781728766997

Dedication

*I dedicate this book to my family,
and to all families who live with the reality of
disabling medical, psychiatric and emotional
health conditions.*

Contents

SCHOOL ACCOMMODATIONS i
SCHOOL ACCOMMODATIONS iii
Foreword xi
On the Importance of an Inclusive World 1
    Start Here: Your Child is Miraculous 2
    Your Child is Normal 3
    FAPE in the LRE: Free and Appropriate Public Education in the Least Restrictive Environment 5
Public Schooling 7
    The Gift of Public Schools 7
    Learning Environments & the Importance of Rules 8
Discover the Rules 11
    Federal Law & Relevant Agencies 12
    State Law 13
    Local Regulations and School District Rules 13
Identify & Document Opportunities for Accommodation 15
    1.   Work with the Student Handbook 15
    2.   Work with the Curriculum Guide 16
    3.   Create a Master List of Necessary Accommodations 17
    Some Context: What an Accommodation Might Look Like 18
    Required Documentation: Healthcare Provider Verification 20
Secure Accommodations 22
    1.   Request for Evaluation 24
    2.   Decision to Proceed Meeting 25
    3.   Consent to Evaluate 25

4.	Evaluation	25
5.	IEP Eligibility Conference	25
6.	IEP Conference	26
7.	IEP Document	27

What's in a Name?: 504 v. IEP 28

Life Beyond High School 29

Appendix 1: Medical Summary Template 31

Appendix 2: Master List of Possible Necessary Accommodations 35

Appendix 3: Doctor Verification Note 41

Appendix 4: Sample Letter to Request Evaluation for Accommodations and Services 43

Appendix 5: Useful Web Page URLS 47

About Mari 49

FOREWORD

My children live with Ehlers-Danlos Syndrome (EDS), a largely invisible disease. While they are generally as beautiful and talented as any other child, they also experience disabling symptoms associated with the syndrome. In their lives, these symptoms can flare up unpredictably, making it very difficult to conform to every academic and behavioral expectation set by their schools.

I have been surprised by how disruptive it has been to live with EDS, and even more so by how difficult the world is about accommodating the complications of living with EDS. In my work with other families with other underlying conditions, I have discovered that any child who needs the school to "work with them" will share similar surprise and frustration.

Over time, I learned how assertive and proactive I needed to be with schools so that my children have the opportunities to develop into the amazing adults that they are destined to be. Without my intentional use of the many legal protections available, my children would have been locked out of the many remarkable educational experiences available through our public schools. I wrote this book to share my knowledge and my processes with families who are on similar journeys through the educational system.

While this book does discuss the laws that protect students with disabilities, please be advised that this book does not constitute legal advice. To help you navigate your child's specific situation, you will want to engage a competent attorney who is familiar with education law and management of complex medical conditions. If my services might be helpful to your educational journey, please contact me through my webpage, at www.MariFranklinLaw.com/contact.html.

School Accommodations

ON THE IMPORTANCE OF AN INCLUSIVE WORLD

With this book, you are starting a journey to make the make sure that school is an inclusive place for your child.

Making the world a more accommodating and inclusive place is an important societal goal. We do our part by successfully securing necessary and reasonable educational accommodations for our children, and in doing so we make our world a better place in several important ways:

- Better for our children to achieve their academic potential.
- Better for educators who work so hard to develop and deliver the best possible learning experience.
- Better for the school community which learns that visible and invisible disabilities don't define a student's potential, as long as the community delivers the reasonable accommodations that remove unreasonable barriers to achievement.
- Better for all of us as we develop the assertiveness needed to express when things are not right, and the collaborative communication skills to find ways to make things right together.

The process of securing educational accommodations is governed by laws. This process provides parents of all children a just and equitable way to define the characteristics of an appropriate education for each child, and to define reasonable accommodations and mandated services that provide a way for that child to access their education.

On the Importance of an Inclusive World

Start Here: Your Child is Miraculous

Never forget that your child's worth is not defined by disabilities. Your child is your miracle. Whatever disabling conditions are part of your child's medical history, these disabling conditions are just one part of your child's reality. Here is a chart that I hope will help you be mindful of the many wonderful things about your child. Please fill out this chart and take a few minutes to bask in how much you love your child. It is an important centering tool as you prepare to advocate for your child.

People My Child Loves	
Things My Child Loves to Do	
Ways My Child Loves to Play	
Books My Child Loves	
Something My Child Does that Makes Me Proud	
Nice Stuff that People Say about My Child	
Something I Think My Child is Really Good At	
People who Love My Child	

On the Importance of an Inclusive World

Good People I Know Because of My Child	
Good Things I Experienced Because of My Child	
Stuff I Appreciate because of My Child	

Always remember these things.

Your child is not defined by the symptoms, the complications, the doctor appointments or all the other stuff that your healthcare team helps you manage. If you are like me, there are a lot of conditions and doctors to manage. I've created the form at Appendix 1 for you to track your doctors, diagnosed and suspected conditions as well as the medications and treatments currently in place. Use that form as a useful tool to keep some of the more important details easily available.

However, never allow yourself or anyone else to use the form at Appendix 1 to define your child. Your child is defined by their humanity, not by their medical record. Because managing medical conditions and reasonable accommodations can be almost a soul-crushing task, remember to regularly center yourself on how much you love your child to maintain a positive perspective throughout this process.

Your Child is Normal

It can be incredibly upsetting to us parents when we discover that our children are not "normal." No matter how hard your child tries, they are not able to comply with most the rules for most of the time. No amount of encouragement, begging, consequences, or discussion will result in your child conforming to the school expectations that all the other children seem to manage without effort.

Even as their most loyal supporters, we can get frustrated when something that seems "trivial" – such as sitting still, keeping hands to themselves, following instructions or participating in singing a song - can create conflict that disrupts the learning environment. At the same time, we can feel angry that the school is unfairly penalizing our child for being unable to conform to behavioral and learning expectations when we know that these things are difficult for our children. We feel guilty for wishing our child was more "normal" while we are furious that the whole system seems "rigged" against our child's success.

Slow down. It's all right to be sad that your child faces barriers in their functional capabilities. It's okay to feel frustrated when teachers, administrators and other parents place unreasonable expectations on your child. It's normal to feel angry about the whole situation.

So, take a deep breath.

Your child is miraculous, beautiful, and ... normal.

Normal for a child who lives with the same medical conditions. Normal for a child who has similar disabling symptoms from a variety of underlying conditions. Normal for a child who is unique in all the world. Embrace your child's normal and rejoice that your child's normal is normal.

The real problem for your child is that the school rules were written with an expectation of a differently normal student. There was never an intention to exclude your child. With this book's guidance, your task is to incorporate your child's normal into your school's expectations of normal and acceptable behaviors. With good communication and planning, you and your child's educational team can create the environment that accepts your child's normal so that your child is able to participate fully in the school community.

FAPE in the LRE:
Free and Appropriate Public Education in the Least Restrictive Environment

Your child is a beautiful being whose existence is miraculous and who will develop into a marvelous adult. As the parent, you have the right and the responsibility to defend your child's right to become a productive member of the learning community and to grow into a productive member of society. You do that by ensuring that your public school delivers a Free and Appropriate Public Education (FAPE) in the Least Restrictive Environment (LRE) to your child.

Your child has a federally protected, legal right to their FAPE in the LRE. Reasonable accommodations and special services are the tools available for you and your child's educators to ensure that disabilities do not interfere with delivering the appropriate education to your child.

On the Importance of an Inclusive World

PUBLIC SCHOOLING

This book deals specifically with your child's rights in the publicly-funded school system in the United States of America. The methods for securing appropriate accommodations are generally the same with private institutions, although some non-public educational systems are not obligated by law to provide accommodations. Dealing with other kinds of school systems is the subject of a different book. Please contact me if you would like me to write about dealing with other kinds of schools.

The Gift of Public Schools

Our children benefit greatly from attending public schools. They make friends, learn to negotiate disagreements and celebrate group accomplishments. They learn institutional rules, how to live within the lines and how to navigate and resolve missteps. They learn how to learn, the most effective ways to study and how to turn in quality work on time. In short, they live in a community of teachers and peers, growing in knowledge and in their capacity to learn, making significant progress towards adulthood.

Learning Environments & the Importance of Rules

To create and maintain an orderly environment conducive to learning, schools impose a lot of rules. Rules about being in the hallways; access to bathrooms; being in class on time; following instructions from teachers, aides and administrators; participating in classroom activities; participating in specials like art, music and physical education; doing your homework; keeping your hands to yourself; using your inside voice; never running with scissors and so on. So many rules. Why so many rules?

Schools are large institutions. According to the National Center for Education Statistics, there are about 50 million students attending almost 100 thousand schools in the United States. That means that there are an average of 500 students per school. In actuality, there tend to be fewer students per building at the elementary level than at the high school level; and there are several very large high schools with over 2,000 students per building. That schools are generally large institutions matters; if I took 500 kids into my home today, chaos would immediately ensue. We don't want our schools to be chaotic places.

The only way for order to prevail in a large learning environment is to be very clear about community expectations. Being good citizens in the classroom, the hallways and at assemblies is reasonably expected of every student. In creating these rules, schools have made assumptions about physical, emotional and behavioral standards that can be expected of every student.

Parents of children with disabilities know that our children belong in the community. To make that happen, we tend to be very creative in finding ways for our children to participate in life. This is good because our children have opportunities to live fully in community with others. At the same time, we get so good at accommodating our children, that we forget all the work and attention that went into establishing our children's successful relationships. We forget that there are many children who do not need these accommodations to participate fully.

Our reality is that our children need accommodations because the underlying expectations of their physical, emotional and behavioral capabilities do not match the assumptions made by the school rule-makers. When our children are unable to meet the community expectations, they become subject to consequences and punishments that were designed for children who are able to meet these expectations. A lot of thought has gone in to the rules, and schools can be rigid about making exceptions. But when a disability is causing the deviation, the school must make reasonable accommodations.

Why? Because it's right. But also because there are rules and laws created by the federal government that protect our children from these unintentionally discriminatory rules. Every child has a right to their Free and Appropriate Public Education in the Least Restrictive Environment, and when school rules hinder that access, our children must be reasonably accommodated. Let's look at how these rules work.

Public Schooling

DISCOVER THE RULES

As a publicly funded government organizations, American schools are governed by rules. Lots of them. Rules that few people bother to study in their entirety. Rules that come from different sources, and that may conflict with one another. Some rules that are completely under the control of the teacher, others that are completely out of the hands of local officials.

In the case of protecting our children's access to their public education, the laws that protect our children come from the federal government. These are rules that cannot be overridden by state law, district policy or school handbooks. Where there are conflicts in this area, the federal law must be obeyed.

Why do you care? Because sometimes there are local rules that end up having a discriminatory effect on our children. And no matter how unintentional the discrimination might be, the local school MUST find a way to neutralize the discriminatory effect of their rule on our children. The law is clear, but it can be a little complicated to apply. For this reason, you might decide to seek the services of an educational advocate or an attorney to help you navigate these issues.

Or you might be able to manage on your own. Let me show you how to find the relevant rules, and how to run the process of securing accommodations, so you can decide if you can handle it on your own.

Federal Law & Relevant Agencies

There are two bodies of federal law that govern how students with disabilities are treated by schools. The first set of laws that are published under the Americans with Disabilities Act (ADA), which requires various federal agencies to prevent discrimination through their own set of laws developed to satisfy Section 504 of the ADA. The second is a set of laws that are published under the Federal Education Act which authorizes both formula and discretionary grants to fund some of the costs related to ensuring access to a FAPE in the LRE.

Protecting students from discrimination is managed by the Office of Civil Rights within the Department of Education. Ensuring a student's access to their FAPE in the LRE is managed by the Office of Special Education and Rehabilitative Services (OSERS) and the Office of Special Education Programs (OSEP) within the Department of Education.

Thus, there are three separate offices within the Department of Education that implement and enforce federal protections for your student. You normally will not need to contact these offices to put together an effective set of accommodations and services for your child. But your child's legal rights to accommodations and special services are enforced by these offices when appropriate. More importantly, your child's rights are based in these laws and knowing how to apply these laws to your situation may be helpful in putting together an effective plan.

If you encounter school officials who believe that their school rules override the federal rules, please contact a competent attorney to bring order to your situation. Just like there is a proper "order of operations" in mathematics, there are legal rules for navigating conflicts of laws. Your discussions with the school officials should not be hung up in whether Federal rules apply (they do). Therefore, if there is a misunderstanding about whether your child must be accommodated, you will need support from an knowledgeable attorney.

State Law

Each state has its set of laws and rules that govern how education is delivered to students. For example, Illinois compiled statutes on Education Law provides guidance on how the state will comply with federal educational requirements as well as a statement of the rules that govern delivering education in Illinois. Each state will have its own education law. These laws provide additional rules, such as how many years of any particular subject must be taught in order to earn a high school diploma. The Legal Information Institute of the Cornell Law School maintains a list of state educational laws online at https://www.law.cornell.edu/wex/table_education.

Local Regulations and School District Rules

Local governments, including Counties, Townships and Municipalities (city/town/village) may also have rules reflecting expectations that children attend school. These may be expressed as curfews, truancy laws or other public health rules.

Finally, school districts will have their own rules. These are often found on district and school web pages. Be aware that there are often district rules, building rules, behavioral rules and academic rules. The "front line" rules that teachers and school administrators know and with which they expect compliance will be those that appear in the "Student Handbook" and "Academic (or Curriculum) Handbook."

Now that you have an idea of how to find all the rules, the next step is to figure out which of those rules could cause problems for your student so that you can negotiate through the process that helps protect our children's access to their education.

Discover the Rules

IDENTIFY & DOCUMENT OPPORTUNITIES FOR ACCOMMODATION

Accommodation is a harmless sounding term for what our kids need. It's an extremely accurate description of some of the simple changes that will allow our children to access their education. At the same time, it is a powerful concept that can modify the harmful impact of systemic school rules. The first step in securing appropriate accommodations is to acknowledge which rules will present difficulties in the school setting.

This process can be very troubling for parents who are struggling with a sense of loss over their child's disabilities. Many parents need to mourn over the "normal" that their child will not experience. Many parents will feel frustration over the need to document everything so that their child can be fully included in the school environment; after all, parents of children without disabilities do not need to go through this process.

I am encouraging you to take your time and to be kind to yourself throughout this process. I am going to insist that you follow my process. And I am going to encourage you to pamper yourself a little as you go through this process.

Let's begin.

Identify & Document Opportunities for Accommodations

1. Work with the Student Handbook

Start by getting your hands on a Student Handbook for your school building. In my home school district, a unified district, all eight elementary schools use the same rules; both middle schools use the same rules; and the high school has its set of rules. All these handbooks are available on the district web page for each school. Working with students from all over the country, I have found even the smallest rural districts post their student handbooks online.

Now, print out the entire handbook.

Really, print out the whole thing.

I am serious, you need this on paper.

Now put it in a three-ring binder.

Grab a beverage of your liking, a highlighter, and a pencil, and start reading. Mark up any rule that strikes you as unrealistic for your child to conform with. Don't worry that other kids can manage to comply with the rule, or that you don't know how the rule can be modified. You need to mark up anything that your child will need help to comply with, including anything that will be impossible to comply with. Make your notes right there on the page... "never gonna happen" "will trigger a panic attack" "can't stand still for longer than 12 seconds" "can't walk farther than 20 feet without resting" "bathroom rules will never work" or whatever the issue is. You do not care if your notes seem "normal;" you care that your notes are truthful and thorough.

2. Work with the Curriculum Guide

Many high schools have a separate document for curriculum from the student handbook. If your school has a separate curriculum guide, you need to run the same process:

Identify & Document Opportunities for Accommodations

1. Get a printed copy of the curriculum guide (print it off the web page or get a printed document from the school).
2. Pour yourself a delightful beverage.
3. With a highlighter and pencil, mark up the curriculum guide with notes about why a requirement may present a problem for your child.

Pay special attention to graduation requirements. In order to graduate, there are classes that every student must take. In my home state of Illinois, if you do not take PE, you will not receive a high school diploma.

When the requirements are dictated by State law, school officials may feel that they have limited discretion in waiving requirements. While they are correct about the importance of state requirements, you are also correct that there has to be a way for the child who cannot safely participate in PE to graduate anyway. After all, federal laws protecting students with disabilities trump state laws on graduation requirements, right?

As it turns out, if your child is unable to fulfill a graduation requirement because of a disability, there are processes to have those requirements waived. In the case of a PE waiver, our school has a process to receive a medical waiver. Through the process of establishing accommodations and services for my children, I was plugged in to the proper process to receive a medical waiver, allowing us to proactively manage the details that would result in a high school diploma.

3. Create a Master List of Necessary Accommodations

Once you have marked up the school handbook and curriculum guide, it is time to create the document that will help you drive the process for reasonable accommodations. Use the chart in Appendix 2 to create a master list of the school rules that will create difficulties for your child.

Identify & Document Opportunities for Accommodations

You want to list everything that could be a problem. This is not the time to hold back and "wait and see" if there will be a problem. Remember that school rules should normally be treated as non-negotiable. School administrators expect that your student will always comply with these rules, or else face consequences. Your list will help guide your educational team through the situations where your child's disabilities will require reasonable accommodations or supportive services.

Be mindful that school rules do a great job of maintaining order, and we are committed to maintaining order so that everyone can learn. But when the rules prevent your child from being able to learn, we need to identify the troublesome rules, identify what our children will be able to do and to secure school accommodations defining the appropriate alternative approach for our children.

Creating this list can make you feel angry, upset, panicky, and a whole host of other unpleasant emotions. Take frequent breaks to take a deep breath. And refer back to the page where you listed things that you love about your child. We are making this list to neutralize the effect of school rules that will get in your child's way, so that, instead of fighting the rules, your child spends school days learning and growing.

Some Context:
What an Accommodation Might Look Like

Working with accommodations can seem a little mysterious. There is actually very little mystery and a boatload of practicality to accommodations. While it is impossible to be exhaustive, this short discussion should help you feel comfortable that you are qualified to create the initial proposed list of accommodations.

Here are some kinds of situations that might need to be accommodating:

- There is never enough time during passing periods for your child to make it to the next class in time.

Identify & Document Opportunities for Accommodations

- Your child never manages to turn in their homework, even when it is done.
- Your child impulsively calls out answers or asks questions during class.
- Your child never participates in class.
- Your child regularly runs out of time to complete tests, even when prepared and knowledgeable about the tested material.
- Your child gets headaches or stomach aches or is otherwise unwell enough to attend class consistently.

Here are some kinds of accommodations that might be helpful to your child's educational success:

- Extra time to pass, including permission to arrive a little late to class without being marked tardy.
- Resource period to help organize school work, and to turn in completed work to the resource teacher.
- Behavioral coaching, including work with a school social worker, to develop classroom appropriate behaviors.
- Refraining from penalizing student for inappropriate classroom behaviors, recognizing that these are works in progress.
- Extra time to complete tests and the option to use an alternate test environment if regular test rooms are too distracting for your student. Note that the provision of this option does not require your child to use it for every test.
- For students whose conditions cause frequent school absences, you may need to establish services of a district-provided homebound tutor.

I've provided this list to give you a sense that there are ways to address all kinds of difficulties. However, I want to emphasize that it is not your job to know all the ways I which your child can be accommodated.

Your job is to identify all the ways in which your child may have difficulty conforming to the school's expectations. With your list as a starting point, your educational team can help create the accommodations and services

Identify & Document Opportunities for Accommodations

that will address the concerns on your list. I'll walk you through creating your list in the next sections.

Required Documentation: Healthcare Provider Verification

Schools will ask for proof that your child has a health condition that requires accommodation. To that end, you will be asked to provide verification of underlying conditions, effect on daily living and effect on ability to access Free and Appropriate Public Education (FAPE) in the Least Restrictive Environment (LRE). The verification is expected to be from one or more medical practitioners.

Use the charts in Appendix 1 & 2 to keep yourself and your medical team organized. Ideally, your pediatrician/PCP is keeping records on the work of each specialist and will be willing to write a letter verifying the need for the accommodations as detailed in your chart. Alternatively, you can have various specialists verify portions of your list as appropriate.

Be aware that these letters take the medical provider quite a bit of time to put together. I recommend making an appointment for the sole purpose of reviewing your child's needs for accommodations, and to provide your doctor enough information to create a note that says something along the lines of the sample note included in Appendix 4.

Important note: if your doctor is not willing to write this note for you, you may need to find yourself a new doctor. In my experience, I have had doctors tell me that they do not want to take legal responsibility for requesting school accommodations. I don't understand what they are talking about. The doctor notes that we need simply are verification from a medical professional that your child has the conditions described, and that these medical conditions can make fulfilling school policy expectations difficult or impossible. The actual accommodations and services provided

Identify & Document Opportunities for Accommodations

will be determined by collaborative meetings between you and school officials.

Identify & Document Opportunities for Accommodations

SECURE ACCOMMODATIONS

Now that you have your information in order and your medical documentation lined up, you are ready to have a productive set of meetings with your school team. This process may seem to be overly complicated or confusing, but it pays to keep on top of it and to accept the safeguards built into the process.

There are a few basic steps to initialize accommodations for your child. There are specific protocols that must be followed for everyone's protection. Every step forward requires you to officially consent to and authorize proceeding to the next step; there is no part of this process that takes decision-making away from the parent.

This leads to seemingly silly steps that effectively ask you if you authorize the school to proceed with your request. Just go along with it and sign what they need to track the process. There are reasons that these safeguards are in place; just be grateful that you don't need to know why these protections are necessary for some students.

Also note that this process can take half a school year (or more) to complete! Out of a 180-day school year, the process is routinely allowed to take up to 94 school days:

- 14 school days between your Request for Evaluation to your first Decision to Proceed meeting,
- Documentation milestone: the district and you decide to proceed AND you authorize the school to evaluate your child
- 60 school days to complete the evaluation (after paperwork is completed with decision and with your authorization).

Secure Accommodations

- The evaluation results must be presented by the 60th school day during an IEP Eligibility Conference.
- If the child is deemed eligible, then IEP accommodations are determined during and IEP Meeting (sometimes held on the same day as the Eligibility Conference; sometimes scheduled as a separate meeting up to 30 school days later).

And the school may request time extensions, which you don't have to grant, but might be in your interest to grant.

Schools are required to take the time to investigate and evaluation the situation in order to determine eligibility and to help determine appropriate accommodations. This is a large undertaking by you and by the school. The procedures to evaluate your requests for accommodations take substantial time and resources for the school to consider. The lists that you worked so hard to compile at Appendix 1 & 2 provide valuable information to help the school acquire all the relevant information necessary to make good decisions about your child's need for accommodations and services.

I have personally never had the process take that long, because I have always had all the analysis and supporting documentation available for the school's use in evaluating my cases. Schools do have diagnosticians and other professional evaluators available, but many are difficult to schedule in a timely manner because of their other day-to-day school responsibilities. This is why any professionally produced documentation by your healthcare providers can be great asset in keeping the school's evaluation process running smoothly and more quickly.

The documentation you provide might be a letter similar to the one in the appendix, or it might be a standard diagnostic report such as a neuropsychological evaluation from a reputable behavioral health hospital. The key is that it must include sound medical or psychological diagnoses, a description of how these conditions interfere with activities of daily living, and specifically request school accommodations to enable the student to fully participate in their educational process.

The school is entitled to accept these reports instead of running its own duplicative evaluation and assessment, thus greatly cutting down the time needed to complete the evaluation process. You do want the school's professionals involved in your process, so be sure to authorize school professionals to confer directly with your healthcare team.

Now that you have a healthy respect for the all the work that goes into your child's accommodations and services, one last note: make your initial accommodations plan as complete as possible. Make sure it includes "every little thing" that could be difficult "sometimes." Through this process, you will meet the school's accommodations and services dream team, a team that comes together in one place specifically to work out ensuring your child's FAPE in the LRE. The best thinking happens when they are all together, so get all your concerns handled at once, so that you are not constantly re-initiating this giant process for "just one more thing."

1. Request for Evaluation

The first step to secure accommodations is a "Request for Evaluation," a letter similar to the one included in Appendix 5, which you will write. Keep a copy for your records, and mail or hand deliver the letter to the school. Within 14 school days of your request, you will have a "Decision to Proceed" meeting with school officials.

2. Decision to Proceed Meeting

During the Decision to Proceed meeting, the district will review your request and supporting materials to determine whether additional evaluation is needed for an eligibility determination. Most schools have professional diagnosticians available for these evaluations, some who may attend this meeting. The meeting is to determine the scope of additional evaluations that the school will undertake in order to determine whether accommodations or services are justified.

3. Consent to Evaluate

At the Decision to Proceed meeting, if additional evaluations are deemed necessary, be sure to consent in writing to those evaluations before you leave the building. Until the school secures your consent, they cannot begin the evaluation process.

4. Evaluation

Once the school has your consent, the school has up to 60 school days for district personnel to complete their evaluations. By the 60th day, the district must hold an IEP Eligibility Conference to review the results of their evaluations, and to determine whether your student is eligible for accommodations and services.

5. IEP Eligibility Conference

The next meeting between the parents and the school is the IEP Eligibility Conference. The sole purpose of this meeting sole is to determine whether your student is eligible for 504 accommodations or IEP special services. If the answer is no, you will be provided an explanation of why that is the case, and you are entitled to appeal the decision. If the answer is yes, the next step is to hold an IEP Conference to determine specific accommodations and services that will be provided to your child.

6. IEP Conference

As a technical matter, the meeting to discuss actual accommodations is a separate meeting from the one when you and the administration come to the determination that your student is entitled to accommodations and services. It can seem like an out-of-body experience that the meeting that determines whether accommodations and services are appropriate is a separate meeting from determining what accommodations and services will be provided. Especially for the schools that adjourn after the eligibility meeting and set the conference meeting for a different day.

Take a deep breath.

Do let the administration know that you are prepared to have both meetings on the same day, one right after the other. A well-organized school district will have used the 60 day evaluation period to provide all the data needed to determine both, eligibility and appropriate accommodations and services. Other schools may need an additional 30 days to complete evaluations to provide enough data to determine appropriate accommodations and services.

Keep your cool if your school is one of the schools that simply do not do both meetings on the same day.

As long as you are moving the process forward, look upon the progress as victory.

And keep to their process. Remember that schools (even small ones) are large institutions that have figured out their method for keeping order. Forcing them to change their method can be really risky. If the change in method causes them to lose track of the process, you may end up needing to re-do parts of the process just to get it back into their method. Keep the giant happy. As long as it is moving forward, do it according to their method.

7. IEP Document

During the IEP Conference, you are collaboratively drafting the documents that establish your child's legal right to certain accommodations and special services. You bring your list to the conference to make sure that you don't miss anything. Be prepared to significantly massage your list into the school's document format. The issues that you have identified should be addressed during the meeting; if you run out of time, you have the right to request additional meeting sessions to cover all of your concerns.

I have found educators and administrators to be remarkable resources in helping our children find ways to fully access their educational opportunities. Most IEP meetings I have attended include many professionals, including special education administrators, case managers, nurses, physical therapists, occupational therapists, counselors, psychologists, social workers and teachers. In most cases, these individuals all know (or will know) your child personally. They are all there to ensure that the school puts forward its best thinking to ensure that your child successfully accesses their FAPE in the LRE.

You should always attend these meetings with a "second," whether the second be an advocate, attorney or bestie. You need someone who will help make sure that all your concerns are adequately and fairly addressed, to help you keep your cool during a rather intense meeting and to make sure that you make the best use of the valuable school team time. You should make sure that suggested accommodations and services are likely to be effective, and that there is a reasonable plan to review the effectiveness of the plan.

An accommodations plan should be considered a "living" document. Strategies that prove ineffective should be reviewed and revised as needed.

IEP goals that are progressing should be noted and adjusted as goals are met. Ideally, you should plan to meet annually with your team to ensure that your accommodations are effective and that they evolve over time as your child develops toward adulthood.

What's in a Name?: 504 v. IEP

In some cases, your educational team will determine that your child does not meet the requirements for an IEP plan, but that 504 accommodations are still appropriate. Should that happen, many schools will follow the same IEP process to create a 504 Accommodations Plan.

Periodically, I see social media debates where parents claim that an IEP is better than a 504, or vice versa. What the plan is called is less important than to secure all accommodations and services necessary for your child to access their FAPE in the LRE. Your school will have their preference for what to call the plan; as long as the plan satisfies your requirements, go with whatever the school calls it.

As a matter of administrative law, the cost of school accommodations provided under Section 504 law of the ADA are borne entirely by your local school. In contrast, the costs of IEP services provided under IDEA are eligible for federal reimbursement. In reality, our children receive a mixture of Section 504 accommodations and IDEA IEP services. To simplify their administration, schools tend to provide either a 504 or an IEP plan for each student. Let the school name the plan.

I have heard parents claim that only an IEP or only a 504 "follows" a child to college or into the workforce. While either document is useful history of your child's accommodations, as a technical matter, neither "follows" your child anywhere. With each new institution -- whether it be educational, vocational, or professional -- your child will need to learn the new process and secure accommodations according to the new process. Learning to do your 504/IEP plan well is a terrific dress rehearsal for the next stage in life after high school.

LIFE BEYOND HIGH SCHOOL

School accommodations and services are important tools to help children with disabilities develop into successful adults. Indeed, the process to identify the need for accommodations and the participation of many dedicated professionals in the school environment can be a great blessing. You have an intentional process to celebrate your child's gifts and to develop appropriate educational plans that will help them succeed academically.

Throughout the public school years, your child's participation in the planning and evaluation processes will increase as their abilities to contribute increase. Early in your child's academic career, you are the critical leader to ensure your child's access to their Free and Appropriate Public Education (FAPE) in the Least Restrictive Environment (LRE). You and the school team will set accommodations and goals, document progress and adjust accommodations and services as your child's capabilities change. Your child's participation in these meetings should increase as they progress through Middle School and High School, as they increasingly take ownership over their learning and their own goals in life.

By high school your child might function as a leader during these meetings. These are critical life skills for all people to develop in order to fully participate in life. After high school, your child's options might involve college, trade schools, apprenticeships or additional training in life skills through the Department of Rehabilitative Services. Some of these options are new life chapters, while others might be additional sections to the high school chapter. Contact your school counselor, case manager or similar professional to explore and plan for these options.

Life Beyond High School

APPENDIX 1: MEDICAL SUMMARY TEMPLATE

The table on the following pages is designed to organize your medical information in a way that provides complete information when you need to share it with the school or with other medical professionals. You should read and fill in the table across the two-page width for best results. Keep this list up to date so that you have a convenient reference available when you meet with school officials or other medical professionals.

School Accommodations
Appendix 1: Medical Summary Template

Specialty Name of Doctor	Address Phone Fax
Pediatrician/ PCP	
Genetics	
Neurology	
Cardiology	
Allergy	
Rheumatology	
Physical Therapy	

School Accommodations
Appendix 1: Medical Summary Template

Conditions Treated	Prescriptions, Therapies & Treatments Prescribed

Make copies as needed.

School Accommodations
Appendix 1: Medical Summary Template

APPENDIX 2: MASTER LIST OF POSSIBLE NECESSARY ACCOMMODATIONS

I developed the table on the following pages to be a tool to help you track and organize your thoughts as you review school policies and procedures. You should read and fill in the table across the two-page width for best results. The goal of this table is to bring as much certainty to your child's school experience as possible, by candidly identifying rules that will be difficult for your child.

The school officials are the experts in what it takes to run a school. You are the expert in how your child is likely to respond in the school environment.

Everyone shares the goal of delivering your child's FAPE in the LRE. This chart is intended to help the team identify potential barriers to doing so, giving the team an opportunity to anticipate issues and build processes that will help your child gracefully overcome the barriers. The best solutions will hold your child reasonably accountable while building experiences and skills that contribute to your child's successful independence.

School Accommodations
Appendix 2: Master List of Possible Necessary Accommodations

Student Name: DOB: Student ID:

School Rules		Accommodations Requested
Page	Rule	Describe Difficulty in Complying (Condition / Limitations)

School Accommodations
Appendix 2: Master List of Possible Necessary Accommodations

Accommodations Requested	
Describe Accommodation Suggested	Verifying Doctor (s)

Make copies as needed.

School Accommodations

Appendix 2: Master List of Possible Necessary Accommodations

Student Name: DOB: Student ID:

School Rules		Accommodations Requested
Page	Rule	Describe Difficulty in Complying (Condition / Limitations)

School Accommodations
Appendix 2: Master List of Possible Necessary Accommodations

Accommodations Requested	
Describe Accommodation Suggested	Verifying Doctor (s)

Make copies as needed.

School Accommodations

Appendix 2: Master List of Possible Necessary Accommodations

APPENDIX 3: DOCTOR VERIFICATION NOTE

This is a sample letter to provide to your doctor to support your request for accommodations.

Consider making an appointment just to review your documentation with your doctor, so that they have sufficient time to ask questions and make recommendations.

The letter allows the doctor to review your master list, affirm that it all seems reasonable, and to request that the school make appropriate arrangements according to their expertise.

School Accommodations
Appendix 3: Doctor Verification Note

[Date]

[School Name]
[School Address]

Attention: [School Administrator]

Dear [School Administrator]

I am writing in support of the request for accommodations and special services for [Student Name], Date of birth [Student Date of Birth], Student ID # [Student ID #].

[Student Name] has been my patient since [date of first visit]. We are following and treating [Student Name] for the following conditions: [list of conditions].

I have reviewed the attached Master List of Necessary Accommodations created by [Parent Name] and it is my opinion that [Student Name]'s health conditions justify the provision of the listed accommodations. I have initialed and dated the list to verify that I have reviewed it.

Please provide accommodations and services to [Student Name] that will ameliorate the difficulties identified in the list. I have done my best as a medical doctor to describe appropriate accommodations. However, I defer to your judgement as professional educators and administrators to adjust the proposed accommodations to ensure operational feasibility in the school environment.

If there are additional questions, please contact my office at [phone number].

Sincerely,

[Doctor Signature]

[Doctor Name & Address or Office Stamp]

APPENDIX 4: SAMPLE LETTER TO REQUEST EVALUATION FOR ACCOMMODATIONS AND SERVICES

This letter to your school administrator establishes your request for an evaluation for accommodations and services and provides authorization to proceed with any evaluations that the school believes appropriate.

Some parents may prefer to pick and choose which evaluations to authorize. If that is the case with you, then delete that sentence from your initial letter.

School Accommodations
Appendix 4: Sample Letter to Request Evaluation

[Today's Date]

[Your Name]
[Your Address]
[City, State ZIP]
[Daytime Telephone]

[Name of Principal or Special Education Administrator]
[Name of School],
[Street Address]
[City, State, ZIP]

Dear [Principal's or Administrator's name],

I am writing to request that my [son/daughter], [child's name], be evaluated for 504 accommodations and for IEP special education services. [Child's name] is in the [grade level] grade at [name of school]. [Teacher's name] is [his/her] teacher.

[Child's name] has been identified as having the following disabilities:

1. [name of disability] by [name of professional].
2. [name of disability] by [name of professional].
3. [name of disability] by [name of professional].

Enclosed are copies of the reports I have received that help describe [child's name]'s condition.

I have also prepared a Master List of Necessary Accommodations and have reviewed it with [Child's name]'s doctors. We have created this document as a starting point for discussion with the school administrative and teaching team. It is my hope that the attached documentation will provide sufficient evaluative information to proceed directly to an Eligibility Conference & IEP meeting. However, if additional evaluation by school diagnosticians is deemed necessary, I

School Accommodations
Appendix 4: Sample Letter to Request Evaluation

hereby give written permission in order for [child's name] to be evaluated.

I look forward to your prompt attention to my request. I will contact you within a week to schedule our first meeting regarding this matter.

Sincerely,

[Your name]

Cc: [Principal], [teachers]

APPENDIX 5: USEFUL WEB PAGE URLS

Americans with Disabilities Act (ADA) - https://www.ada.gov/cguide.htm

Federal Education Act -https://sites.ed.gov/idea/statuteregulations/

Office of Special Education and Rehabilitative Services (OSERS) - https://www2.ed.gov/about/offices/list/osers/index.html

Office of Special Education Programs (OSEP) - https://www2.ed.gov/about/offices/list/osers/osep/about.html

Illinois compiled statutes on Education Law - http://www.ilga.gov/legislation/ilcs/ilcs4.asp?ActID=1005&ChapterID=17&SeqStart=155000000&SeqEnd=157450000

The Legal Information Institute of the Cornell Law School maintains a list of state educational laws online at https://www.law.cornell.edu/wex/table_education.

HIPAA Privacy Rules - http://www.hhs.gov/ocr/privacy/hipaa/administrative/privacyrule/privruletxt.txt

www.MariFranklinLaw,com

ABOUT MARI

I am an attorney, an independent college counselor, an information scientist and a mother.

As in-house counsel, my early legal work covered patents, trademarks, copyrights, contracts, legal jurisdictional issues and transactional negotiations for cutting-edge computer technologies companies. Through my work, I bridged the communications gap between computer-based technologists, business teams, legal teams and our customers.

Fast forward to being mom. A rare medical disorder inherited by my children became the cause of hundreds of medical appointments, tests and corresponding school absences as their symptoms developed. The medical condition was severely affecting my children's ability to participate in school, and I discovered that I needed to become an expert in the laws that protect their rights to public education.

These protections require working several levels of federal, state, and local law, including complex Federal laws such as the Americans with Disabilities Act, the Individuals with Disabilities Education Act and HIPAA Privacy Rules, which each affect how we communicate and what we decide. And the work involves many people, including parents, therapists, doctors, school educators, school nurses, school intervention specialists and school administrators. My understanding of how all these laws interact to assure my children's right to a free appropriate public education in the least restrictive environment was critical in getting everything working smoothly.

My education includes degrees from Hunter College High School in New York City; the University of Chicago; and the Illinois Institute of

About Mari

<u>Technology / Chicago-Kent School of Law</u>. My work experience includes IEP/504 advocacy, educational consulting, corporate law and administration; computer technology user interface design, system implementation, system training, and programming; macro- and micro-economic research and analysis; and marketing communications.

My life experience as a mother, community leader and church volunteer has sharpened my focus on the unique gifts of each child, which must be part of any child's educational plan. Our responsibility is to raise our children into successful adults. I am available for legal advice through my website at <u>www.MariFranklinLaw.com</u>

Made in the USA
Columbia, SC
07 July 2019